My Name is Nina!

English Conversations for Kids

Teacher's Guide

Natalia Bochorishvili
Vitalij Palkus

My Name is Nina!

English Conversations for Kids

Teacher's Guide

Natalia Bochorishvili
Vitalij Palkus

Addison-Wesley Publishing Company

A publication of the World Language Division

Editorial Development: Karen Howse
Layout and Production: Karen Howse
Cover Photograph: Zane Williams
Additional illustrations: Andrej Kouleshov and Iskra Kouleshova
Manufacturing: James W. Gibbons

ISBN: 0-201-83264-X
1 2 3 4 5 6 7 8 9 10-CRS-00 99 98 97 96

Contents

Unit 1	Hello. Is Nina there?	6-7
Unit 2	Happy birthday!	8-9
Songs	Here We Go Round the Mulberry Bush	8
	If You're Happy and You Know It	8
Unit 3	What are they doing?	10-11
Unit 4	I do it. I'm doing it.	12-13
Unit 5	How are you feeling?	14-15
Unit 6	Let's go together.	16-17
Unit 7	I'll do it tomorrow.	18-19
Unit 8	Would you like...? I'd like...	20-21
Unit 9	Do you have...? I need...	22-23
Unit 10	May I...? Can you...?	24-25
Unit 11	How can I get there?	26-27
Unit 12	I have to...	28-29
Songs	Mary Had a Little Lamb	28
	Twinkle Twinkle Little Star	28
Unit 13	How was your trip?	30-31
Unit 14	He went home.	32-33
Unit 15	How did you like it?	34-35
Unit 16	I was sleeping when...	36-37
Unit 17	I did it. I've done it.	38-39
Unit 18	I think... I don't know.	40-41
Unit 19	He is the best.	42-43
Unit 20	She looks like...	44-45

UNIT 1. Hello. Is Nina there?

Student Book pages 4-5

KEY EXPERIENCES

- Answering the phone
- Asking for somebody on the phone

KEY LANGUAGE

- Hello. Is (Nina) there?
- May I speak to (Jane)?
- Speaking ...
- Just a minute ...
- Hold on, please.
- This is she.
- Sorry, he's out.
- She isn't here.

SUGGESTED ACTIVITIES

1. Play the tape for the telephone conversation at the top of student book page 4. Ask students to repeat the conversation. Then have them work in pairs, making up similar conversations. Give options on how to start, *Hello. Is (Carla) there? or May I speak to (John)?* Also give options on how to respond, *Speaking. This is he/she.*

2. Play the tape for the second conversation. Discuss the difference (here the child is speaking to an adult and the language is more formal). Draw attention to the way hello sounds in the first conversation (when it's a greeting) and hello in the second conversation (when it's a phone pick-up word).

3. Have students work in pairs acting out telephone conversations with a) their own parents; b) their friends' parents; and c) their teachers.

4. Play the tape for page 5. Introduce the new expressions.

5. Have students make up new conversations. Ask them to discuss who is speaking with whom and what they are saying. Encourage the students to make longer conversations rather than stop after the opening phrases.

6. Reproduce the blackline master on page 7 of this guide for each student. Circulate around the class, helping students complete the page if necessary.

Write a telephone conversation between the little astronaut and his friend on earth.

Hello.

Hello. This is _____

_____

I'm fine _____

_____

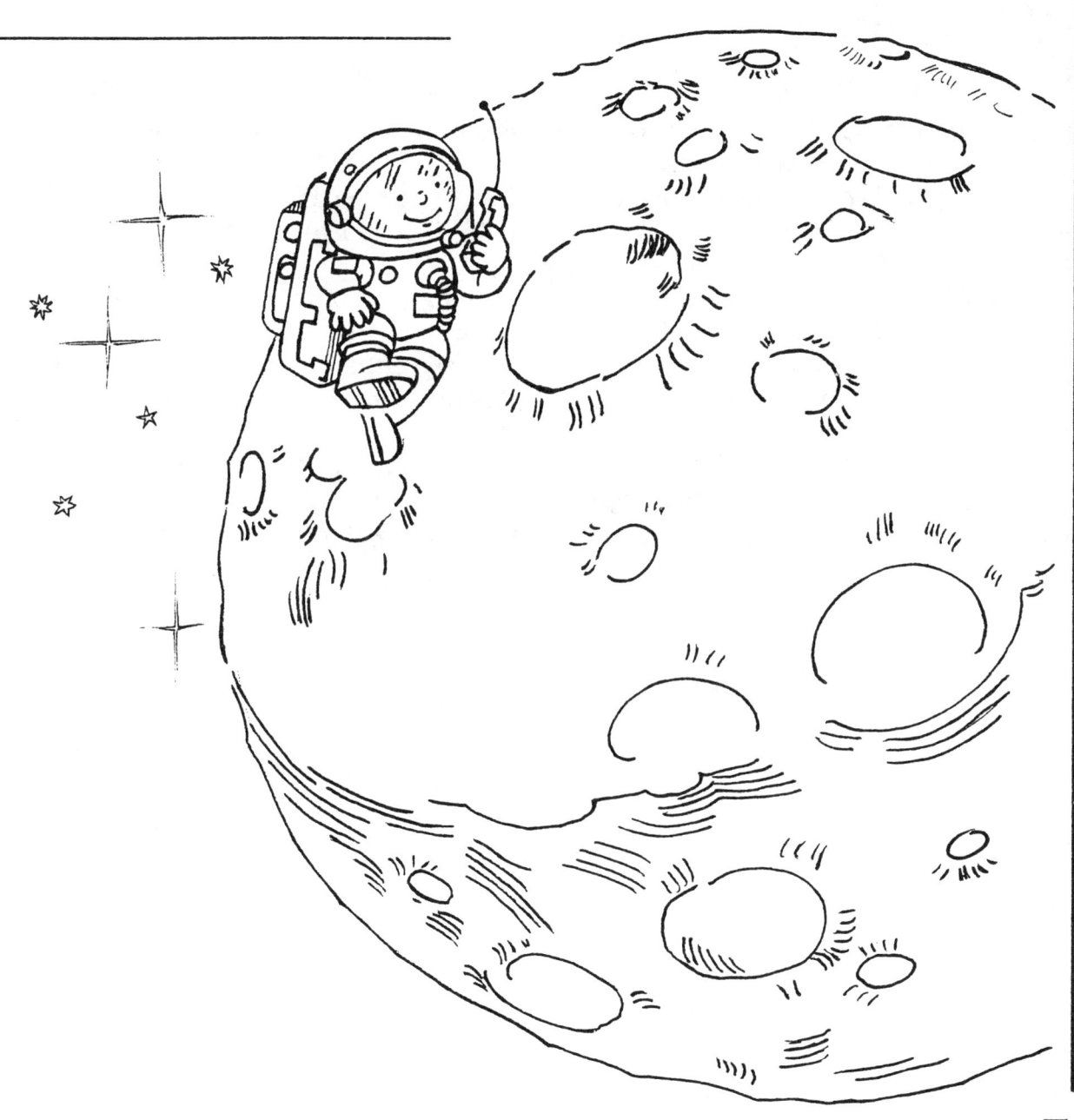

7

UNIT 2. Happy birthday!

Student Book pages 6-7

KEY EXPERIENCES

- Wishing "happy birthday"
- Asking and telling birth dates

KEY LANGUAGE

- Happy birthday!
- Here's a present for you.
- When is your birthday?
- It's in (April).
- I'll be (six) on the (12th of July).

SUGGESTED ACTIVITIES

1. Play the tape for student book page 6 as students follow along in their books. Have them repeat the conversation.
2. Play the tape for student book page 7. Introduce the names of the months. Practice ordinals, 1st/first, 2nd/second, etc. Then tell your birth date, *My birthday is on the 3rd of September.*
3. Have students work in pairs asking and telling their birth dates.
4. Have one student play the role of a birthday boy/girl as the other students come with various birthday presents. They can either use real objects available in the classroom or drawings of imaginary presents. Encourage them to discuss the presents.
5. Reproduce the blackline master on page 9 of this guide for each student. Circulate around the class, helping students complete the page if necessary.
6. Play the tape for the songs on pages 8 and 9 of the student book. Have students listen to the songs and sing along. Return to these songs as often as possible—just for fun.

Write what you would like to wish your parents and friends on these holiday postcards.

9

UNIT 3. What are they doing?

Student Book pages 10-11

KEY EXPERIENCES

- Playing a guessing game
- Describing a circus scene

KEY LANGUAGE

- What are they doing?
- They are (dancing).
- Are they (fighting)?
- sleep, sing, laugh, cry, run, jump, fight, dance
- Present progressive tense

SUGGESTED ACTIVITIES

1. With students' books closed, play the tape for page 10 up to *Are they fighting?* Encourage students to give some suggestions on what is happening.
2. With students' books open, have students give the correct answer. Ask, *Who is dancing? Are they dancing tango/polka/rock 'n' roll?*
3. Play a similar guessing game. Have two students come to the front of the class. Assign the pair an action verb from the box on page 11of the student book to role-play. The rest of the class closes their eyes and tries to guess what the pair is doing. Repeat with different pairs of students.
4. Play the tape for page 11. Have students describe what's happening at the circus. Ask, *Why are some of the kids laughing and some of the kids crying?*
5. Bring some photographs/pictures of people in action to class. Hold up a picture and have students describe what is happening.
6. Reproduce the blackline master on page 11 of this guide for each student. Circulate around the class, helping students complete the page if necessary.

Write about these kids. What are they doing?

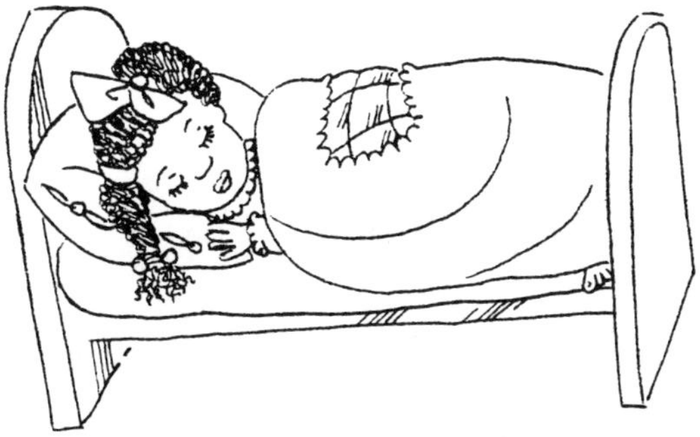

_____
_____

_____
_____

_____
_____

_____
_____

© Addison-Wesley Publishing Company

11

UNIT 4. I do it. I'm doing it.

Student Book pages 12-13

KEY EXPERIENCES

- Discussing activities
- Discussing abilities

KEY LANGUAGE

- I usually (eat ice cream).
- I'm (eating ice cream).
- Does he play (tennis)?
- He's playing (tennis) now.
- usually, at the moment, always, every day, today, often, now

SUGGESTED ACTIVITIES

1. Play the tape for page 12 as students follow along in their books. Discuss the pictures. Ask, *What is the boy doing? Does he like ice cream? Does he eat it often? Does the boy in the picture play tennis? Is he playing it? What is he doing?*, etc.
2. Have two or three students role-play an activity as the class guesses what they are doing, *Are they sleeping?*
3. Discuss the situations on page 13. *She teaches. She gives a geography class. She is getting flowers. She is smiling. The kids go to school... They study. They take classes. They are giving flowers to their teacher. They are wishing her a happy birthday. The man drives a truck. He is a truck driver. He is flying in the balloon.*
4. Reproduce the blackline master on page 13 of this guide for each student. Circulate around the class, helping students complete the page if necessary.

Think of some of your favorite books and write the titles on the book covers.

BOOK 2
My Name is Nina!

BOOK 2
My Name is Nina!
English Conversation for Kids

What are they reading right now?

_____

UNIT 5. How are you feeling?

Student Book pages 14-15

KEY EXPERIENCES

- Discussing health
- Expressing need

KEY LANGUAGE

- What's the matter?/What's wrong?
- I'm (hungry/thirsty/tired/cold).
- I feel sick.
- I don't feel very well.
- I have a cold/a headache.
- Do you need to (go to the bathroom)?

SUGGESTED ACTIVITIES

1. Play the tape for page 14, pausing after each statement for students to repeat.
2. Have students make up short conversations between the characters on page 14.
3. Role-play. Have one student play the role of the doctor, as other students role-play patients and tell about their health problems. The "doctor" listens, asks more questions, and gives the advice.
4. Have students work in pairs to describe the scene on page 15. Then have the pairs make conversations between the teddy-bear doctor and the other animals.
5. Reproduce the blackline master on page 15 of this guide for each student. Circulate around the class, helping students complete the page if necessary.

Write a conversation between the sick boy and his parents.

Father: What's the matter?

Mother: He _____

    and _____ .

Father: How are you feeling now?

Boy: I'm _____ .

    and I'm _____

    I have _____ ,

    and I have _____ .

UNIT 6. Let's go together.

Student Book pages 16-17

KEY EXPERIENCES

- Talking about future plans
- Discussing activities

KEY LANGUAGE

- What are you doing (tomorrow)?
- We're going (skiing). You can join us.
- Let's go to (the park).
- Sounds good to me.
- Present progressive tense

SUGGESTED ACTIVITIES

1. Play the tape for page 16 and have students repeat the conversations in pairs.
2. Ask students to make up similar conversations using their own suggestions for joint activities.
3. Go around the class and talk with students about their plans for the summer/weekend/rest of the day, etc. Ask them to give suggestions for class activities, *Let's listen to some music*, etc.
4. Play the tape for page 17, pausing to have students repeat. Ask them to make conversations with the boys in the picture. To make conversations more varied and interesting, they might reject some of the suggestions and come up with different offers. *Let's watch a movie. No, I don't feel like watching TV. Let's go for a walk.*
5. Reproduce the blackline master on page 17 of this guide for each student. Circulate around the class, helping students complete the page if necessary.

The kids are playing in the forest.
What are they saying to each other?
Write five sentence starting with *Let's* ....

Unit 7. I'll do it tomorrow.

Student Book pages 18-19

KEY EXPERIENCES

• Talking about future actions

KEY LANGUAGE

• Are you going to (wash the dishes) now?
• I'll do it tomorrow.
• We'll go tomorrow.
• I'll (sing a song).

SUGGESTED ACTIVITIES

1. Play the tape for the first conversation on page 18. Ask students to suggest other replies instead of *OK. We'll go tomorrow.* For example, *Let's go today* or *We'll go this afternoon.*

2. Play the tape for the second conversation. Ask students to role-play in pairs and continue the conversation between the girl and her brother, starting with *Are you going to ...*

3. Have students work in small groups and talk about their own plans for the future. Encourage them to use all possible patterns.

4. Play the tape for page 19. Have students work in pairs to make a conversation between Nina and Maria. Then talk about their plans, *Nina is going to clean her room,* etc.

5. Tell students about your plans, *Tonight I'm going to go to the movies.* Then have students tell about their plans.

6. Reproduce the blackline master on page 19 of this guide for each student. Circulate around the class, helping students complete the page if necessary.

The kids are going to take part in a concert.
They are discussing their roles.
Write what each of them is saying about it.

_____

_____

_____

_____

_____

UNIT 8. Would you like...? I'd like...

Student Book pages 20-21

KEY EXPERIENCES

- Expressing wants
- Discussing foods

KEY LANGUAGE

- Would you like (this apple)?
- I'd like (some candy).
- Would you like (to dance)?
- apple, cookie, orange, sandwich, tea, pizza, ice cream
- draw, dance, fly, swim, ride

SUGGESTED ACTIVITIES

1. Play the tape for page 20 and have students repeat the conversations.
2. Go around the class, asking questions starting with, *Would you like (a cookie)?* Have students respond with, *Yes, I would,* or *No, I'd like (an orange).*
3. Have students work in small groups to role-play ordering in a restaurant. One can play the role of a waiter, the others act as the customers. Suggest some phrases, *What would you like for desert,* etc.
4. Play the tape for page 21 as students follow along in their books. Have pairs of students make conversations. Then have the class describe activities they would like to do.
5. Reproduce the blackline master on page 21 of this guide for each student. Circulate around the class, helping students complete the page if necessary.

Read the lines for a famous song by The Beatles.

I'd like to be under the sea,
In an octopus's garden in the shade.
We would shout and swim about,
The coral that lies beneath the waves.
Oh what joy for every girl and boy,
Knowing they're happy and they're safe.

Where would you like to be?

_____

_____

_____

UNIT 9. Do you have...? I need...

Student Book pages 22-23

KEY EXPERIENCES

- Expressing wants and needs
- Discussing money

KEY LANGUAGE

- Do you have (a red pencil)?
- May I borrow it, please?
- What do you need?
- I need (some quarters).
- dollar, quarter, dime, nickel, penny

SUGGESTED ACTIVITIES

1. Play the tape for page 22 as students follow along in their books. Have students work in pairs repeating the conversation.
2. Have students make their own conversations starting with, *Do you have (a crayon)*, and telling about things they have and things they need.
3. Have students make new conversations asking for change, saying how much they need, and what they want to buy.
4. Play the tape for page 23 as students follow along. Talk about some other jobs and things people need at work.
5. Reproduce the blackline master on page 23 of this guide for each student. Circulate around the class, helping students complete the page if necessary.

Which of these do you have?
Which of these do you need but don't have?
Write your answers.

_____

_____

Draw some other objects that you need.
Write four sentences about the things you need.

_____

_____

UNIT 10. May I...? Can you...?

Student Book pages 24-25

KEY EXPERIENCES

• Practicing polite requests/responses

KEY LANGUAGE

• May I ask you something?
• Can you help me?
• Can I sit here?
• What's wrong?
• Modals: can, may

SUGGESTED ACTIVITIES

1. Explain to students that can/could is often used to ask people to do things, *Can you help me?* Can or may is used to ask for permission or to give permission, *Can I sit here? May I ask you something?*

2. Play the tape for the first conversation on page 24 as students follow along. Have student pairs make short conversations starting with, *May I ask you something?*

3. Play the tape for the second conversation on page 24. Have students repeat, but with variations on the girl's problem, *I can't find the way to the station.*

4. Play the tape for the third conversation and have students practice asking for permission. Encourage them to use both can and may.

5. Have students ask for permission to stand up/go out/open the door, etc. Give various responses, *Sure. No, you can't. No way.*, etc.

6. Play the tape for page 25. Ask students to make conversations between Nina and her friends. Then have them role-play the conversations.

7. Reproduce the blackline master on page 25 of this guide for each student. Circulate around the class, helping students complete the page if necessary.

Nina and Jerry want to feed the pony.
They are discussing what they can give the pony to eat.
Write their conversation.

Jerry: _____ a hamburger?

Nina: No, you can't. It _____

_____ an apple?

Jerry: _____

Nina: _____ some grass?

Jerry: _____

UNIT 11. How can I get there?

Student Book pages 26-27

KEY EXPERIENCES

• Asking for and giving directions

KEY LANGUAGE

• Excuse me. How can I get to (West Street)?
• Is it far?
• Can I walk there?
• You can take the (bus).
• turn right, turn left, go straight ahead

SUGGESTED ACTIVITIES

1. Play the tape for page 26. Have students repeat the conversations.
2. Bring various city/state maps to class. Have students work in pairs. Give each pair a different map. Have them ask for and give directions on how to get to certain locations.
3. Have students look at the map on page 27. Students ask for and give directions, *Is there a (restaurant) near here?* Encourage them to ask about other things, (post office, supermarket, movie theater, etc.) that are not in the picture.
4. Reproduce the blackline master on page 27 of this guide for each student. Circulate around the class, helping students complete the page if necessary.

Draw a map of how to get to your house from your school.
Then write the directions.

UNIT 12. I have to...

Student Book pages 28-29

KEY EXPERIENCES

- Declining offers
- Expressing necessity

KEY LANGUAGE

- I have to (do my homework).
- You have to do the work again.
- You made a lot of mistakes.

SUGGESTED ACTIVITIES

1. Explain that have to is used to say that it is necessary to do something. You usually have to do something because of a certain rule or the situation. Model these sentences and have students repeat. *I have to do my homework* (absolutely). *I should do my homework* (it would be good to do it).

2. Play the tape for the first conversation on page 28. Ask students, *Does the boy want to go to a picnic? Why is he saying no?*

3. Have students work in pairs. One student suggests something, *Would you like to (play a game).*, or *Let's (watch TV).*, and the partner gives reasons why he or she can't do it, starting with, *I have to (wash the dishes).*, or *I must (clean my room).*

4. Play the tape for the second conversation on page 28. Explain that *You made a lot of mistakes* and *I did?* are in the past tense.

5. Have students make conversations with, *You have to do the work again.* For example, *Look, the cup is dirty. You have to wash it again.*

6. Play the tape for page 29. Have students work in small groups to do the activity. They should use *have to* or *must/mustn't* either in what the gardener is saying or in what the children are replying. For example, *You have to keep your dog on a leash. I have to catch it first. You mustn't swim in the fountain. Swimming here is prohibited.*

7. Reproduce the blackline master on page 29 of this guide for each student. Circulate around the class, helping students complete the page if necessary.

8. Play the tape for the songs on pages 30 and 31 of the student book. Have students listen to the songs and sing along. Return to these songs as often as possible—just for fun.

Nina is making plans for the day. Help her write down what she has to do.

UNIT 13. How was your trip?

Student Book pages 32-33

KEY EXPERIENCES

• Talking about past experiences

KEY LANGUAGE

• How was your trip?
• It was (terrific)!
• Weren't you afraid?
• Past tense of verb: to be

SUGGESTED ACTIVITIES

1. Play the tape for page 32. Have students talk about the kids. *Are they classmates/neighbors? What did the girl say about the trip?*
2. Ask students to continue the conversation with questions similar to *Weren't you afraid?* such as *Weren't you cold? Cold. Of course not.*
3. Ask students questions. *Where were you yesterday? How was your weekend? How was your vacation?*
4. Have students work in pairs talking about real or imagined trips.
5. Have students discuss some event/party/movie/book starting with, *How was the (parade)?*
6. Play the tape for page 33. Ask students to make up conversations between the man and the woman.
7. Reproduce the blackline master on page 31 of this guide for each student. Circulate around the class, helping students complete the page if necessary.

The three boys are talking about their adventures.
Write a story one of them is telling.

_____

_____

_____

_____

_____

UNIT 14. He went home. ──────────

Student Book pages 34-35

KEY EXPERIENCES

- Discussing a party
- Making up a story

KEY LANGUAGE

- He went home.
- He enjoyed the party.
- We laughed a lot.
- Simple past tense

SUGGESTED ACTIVITIES

1. Explain that regular past tense verbs end in -ed (enjoyed, laughed). Irregular verbs should be memorized (go-went, eat-ate, drink-drank, sing-sang, etc.)
2. Play the tape for page 35. Have students discuss the picture. *Ask, What are the kids doing? What are they saying?* Then have students role-play the conversation.
3. Introduce questions with *did, Did they enjoy the party? Did they dance?* etc.
4. Have students continue the conversation between the three kids, asking and answer the questions.
5. Give students a list of verbs in past tense form. Have students work in small groups making up a story. Each student adds a sentence with one verb from the list. Then one of the students tells the whole story to another group.
6. Play the tape for page 35. Have students make up sentences from the words in the box. They can work in groups choosing characters in the picture and making a sentence. *I ate only ice cream. I didn't want hamburgers*, etc.
7. Reproduce the blackline master on page 33 of this guide for each student. Circulate around the class, helping students complete the page if necessary.

The little dog stayed at home alone. What did he do?
Write about his day using the verbs: *to run, to play,*
to jump, to eat, to drink, to fall asleep.

_____

_____

_____

_____

_____

UNIT 15. How did you like it?

Student Book pages 36-37

KEY EXPERIENCES

- Discussing impressions
- Expressing likes and dislikes

KEY LANGUAGE

- Did you like (the movie)?
- I loved/liked/hated it!
- It was great/super/disgusting!
- nice, cute, funny, great, super, terrific
- disgusting, terrible, scary, mean, horrible

SUGGESTED ACTIVITIES

1. Play the tape for page 36 as students follow along in their books. Ask, *What part did the boy like? What part did the girls like?*

2. Have students work in two groups and discuss a possible plot of the movie. Ask them some questions, *Where did it all happen? When did it happen? Who were the main characters? What did the dragon want?*

3. Have students work in pairs telling their partners about some movies/stories they liked a lot and some that they hated. Encourage them to use words from this unit.

4. Play the tape for page 37. Discuss the titles of the stories and ask students to tell about the characters.

5. Reproduce the blackline master on page 35 of this guide for each student. Circulate around the class, helping students complete the page if necessary.

Draw a scene from your favorite movie on the TV screen.
Write what you like best about the movie.

UNIT 16. I was sleeping when...

Student Book pages 38-39

KEY EXPERIENCES

• Telling a story

KEY LANGUAGE

• Past progressive tense
• Simple past tense
• fighting, jumping, sleeping, playing the piano, playing chess, hiding

SUGGESTED ACTIVITIES

1. Play the tape for page 38 as students follow along in their books. Ask students to describe the monster.
2. Ask, *What was the boy doing? What did the boy say? Did the other boy believe him?*
3. Have students work in groups making up a scary story. Ask them to use the past progressive tense used in the story on page 38. Then have the groups share their stories with the class.
4. Play the tape for page 39. Have students make sentences using the words in the box. Then have them role-play a conversation between the teacher and the kids.
5. Reproduce the blackline master on page 37 of this guide for each student. Circulate around the class, helping students complete the page if necessary.

Write what happened when he was fishing.

He was fishing when.... _____

_____

_____

_____

_____

_____

UNIT 17. I did it. I've done it.

Student Book pages 40-41

KEY EXPERIENCES

• Discussing movies/books
• Expressing likes and dislikes

KEY LANGUAGE

• I saw (Aladdin). Have you seen it?
• I haven't seen it yet.
• I've read the book.
• yesterday, last year, last month, today, this year, this month, already
• Present perfect tense
• Past perfect tense

SUGGESTED ACTIVITIES

1. Ask students, *Have you seen (Aladdin/The Lion King/etc.)? When did you see it?*
2. Explain the use of the present perfect tense. Then play the tape for page 40 as students follow along in their books.
3. Have students make up similar conversations in pairs, discussing movies/cartoons/books, etc.
4. Play the tape for page 41. Have students work in pairs answering the questions.
5. Reproduce the blackline master on page 39 of this guide for each student. Circulate around the class, helping students complete the page if necessary.

Nina and her friends love rides.

Have you been to a place with rides like this one?_____

How many times? _____

When did you go last time? _____

Did you enjoy it? _____

© Addison-Wesley Publishing Company

UNIT 18. I think... I don't know.

Student Book pages 42-43

KEY EXPERIENCES

• Telling suppositions and ideas

KEY LANGUAGE

• I think it's (Rio de Janeiro).
• I guess...
• I believe...
• I don't know.

SUGGESTED ACTIVITIES

1. Play the tape for page 42 as students follow along in their books. Ask students about the capitol of Morocco. Encourage them to make many suggestions.
2. Have students work in pairs, asking more questions about countries/cities/ mountains, etc. Introduce, *I guess... I believe... I suppose...*
3. Start telling students a story, then stop and ask them to guess/give suggestions about what happens next.
4. Play the tape for page 43. Then have students work in pairs answering the questions. Encourage them to use the phrases in the box at the bottom of the page.
5. Reproduce the blackline master on page 41 of this guide for each student. Circulate around the class, helping students complete the page if necessary.

Which is the highest mountain in the world?
Which is the longest river in the world?
Which is the tallest building in the world?
Nina and here friends are trying to answer these questions.
Write a conversation between them about what they think
   the answers are. Use a separate piece of paper.

41

UNIT 19. He is the best.

Student Book pages 44-45

KEY EXPERIENCES

- Using comparisons
- Talking about abilities

KEY LANGUAGE

- Comparatives/superlatives
  good-better-best
  bad-worse-worst
  tall-taller-tallest
  more-most
- ambitious, advanced

SUGGESTED ACTIVITIES

1. Play the tape for page 44 as students follow along in their books. Ask three students to role-play these characters. They can act out a short conversation where each character tells about his/her best abilities.
2. Have students work in small groups to discuss who is the tallest/strongest/ most ambitious, etc. in the class.
3. Have students compare any two kids from the class using, *Jane is taller than Mark.*
4. Ask the following questions, *Who is the fastest runner? Who is better at sports, Tom or Jimmy? Who is the best at soccer in the class?*
5. Have students work in pairs to answer the questions on page 45. Then have them make a conversation between the kids in the picture.
6. Reproduce the blackline master on page 43 of this guide for each student. Circulate around the class, helping students complete the page if necessary.

Write sentences about these animals.
an elephant/a camel (carry heavy things)
a monkey/a bear (climb the tree)
a dolphin/a shark (swim)

UNIT 20. She looks like...

Student Book pages 46-48

KEY EXPERIENCES

- Describing appearances
- Describing clothing

KEY LANGUAGE

- Look what she's wearing!
- She looks like (an exotic bird).
- white, black, red, yellow, blue, green, gray, pink, brown, purple, orange
- dress, skirt, pants, shirt, jacket, blouse, sweater, T-shirt, shorts, cap, shoes, socks

SUGGESTED ACTIVITIES

1. Ask students to describe the girl on page 46. Ask, *How does she look?*
2. Play the tape for page 46. Ask, *Why does she look like an exotic bird? What is she wearing? What color is her hair?*
3. Give students various pictures and photographs of people and ask them to describe their appearances.
4. Ask students to tell about the most beautiful person/character they know and about the ugliest one.
5. Play the tape for page 47. Have students describe Nina's friends.
6. Reproduce the blackline master on page 45 of this guide for each student. Circulate around the class, helping students complete the page if necessary.
7. Play the tape for page 48 of the student book. Have students describe Nina, and say good-bye to her.

Write about Nina and Jerry.
How are they dressed?
Who do they look like?
What are they saying?

_____

_____

_____

_____

_____

_____